Hi Roger,
It was very nice
spending time with
you on Friday. Good luck
In your trip
David Charle

Thanks for
being here
Amy Gerry

Thank you so much
for giving me $100.0
for the Nationals. I
wasn't even expecting
that. God bless you.
— Yelena Roslaya

Best Wishes
Jim & Kim Hammer.

Victoria Kehler
Hybrio

Thanks,
Coleen Andersen

Thanks
Brian Johannson
Canada

Thank you for
coming — I'm delighted
you like our bird.
See you again some day.
Carl Groenwold

OREGON

Wild and Beautiful II

Photography by Dennis Frates

FARCOUNTRY
PRESS

Dedication

To Judy and Nicki for their acceptance and support of my photographic passion. And to Rick whose unending patience allowed many of these photographs to be made.

FRONT COVER: Alpine wildflowers paint a meadow below the snowy slopes of Middle Sister Mountain.

BACK COVER: This shoreline path near Yachats offers stunning views of the Pacific Ocean.

TITLE PAGE: Forest greenery surrounds a well-traveled path at Seal Rock State Park.

RIGHT: Yellow rabbit brush blooms in a valley below Middle Sister and North Sister Mountains in the Three Sisters Wilderness.

PAGE 4: A young great horned owl is camouflaged by an old barn on the Summer Lake State Wildlife Refuge.

PAGE 5: Volcanic ash layers give stripes of color to Oregon's Painted Hills.

ISBN: 1-56037-261-3

© 2004 Farcountry Press

Photographs © 2004 Dennis Frates, unless otherwise indicated

For more information on our books write: Farcountry Press, P.O. Box 5630, Helena, MT 59604, call (800) 821-3874, or visit www.farcountrypress.com

Created, produced and designed in the United States.

Printed in China.

Foreword by Dennis Frates

I have been an avid fly fisherman my entire life. This is one of the reasons I moved to Oregon. In fact, within days of moving here some thirty years ago, while I still had boxes to unload, I set off on my first fishing trip. Since then, I have fly fished throughout the entire state. These trips brought me to Oregon's remote areas, so when I started photographing, it was natural to start there. Now, after photographing Oregon for nearly twenty years, I still find new landscapes and regions I haven't yet explored.

Oregon is one of the most visited states, partly because of its incredible diversity of landscapes. In one day, a visitor can explore monolithic volcanic spires that rise above the rugged, pounding surf along the seashore, pass through idyllic farmland that is the nation's prime producer of grass seed and Christmas trees, tour breathtaking vistas of volcanic mountains, and end the day watching antelope saunter through sagebrush in the eastern part of the state.

Oregon has one national park, Crater Lake, and several world-class destinations, such as the Cascade Mountains, Columbia River Gorge National Scenic Area, and a famous coastline.

Sparkling and clear, Crater Lake gives new meaning to the term "blue water." The Cascade Mountains, rising abruptly many thousands of feet from their nearby base, have been carved into knife-edged peaks by glaciers, some of which still remain on the taller peaks, such as Mt. Hood.

The often-photographed waterfalls of the Columbia River Gorge are nothing short of stunning. It's not hard to spend an entire summer day walking in and around these easily accessible waterfalls. Thunderous torrents of water produce a mist that causes an oasis of green and an intoxicating fresh smell.

Oregon's coastline is one of the most accessible in America. The great majority of its length is open to the public.

Many other lesser-known places in Oregon are equally breathtaking: Steens Mountain, the Wallowa Mountains, and the Summer Lake area, to name just a few. Steens Mountain has several U-shaped, glaciated valleys. The first time I saw these enormous gorges, I was stopped in my tracks by their awesome grandeur. Only the Grand Canyon has evoked a similar response in me. The remote, snow-capped Wallowas are impressive, looming just above the ranching communities of Joseph and Enterprise, while the Summer Lake area contains a wildlife refuge and has more petroglyphs than almost anywhere else in the United States.

It is my sincere hope that those who pick up this book will feel some of the inspiration I felt when making these photographs. Experience a taste of the incredible beauty Oregon has to offer. ✧

ABOVE: Pear tree blossoms come into view as the sun rises over Mt. Hood.

FACING PAGE: Multnomah Falls, one of the tallest waterfalls in the country, drops 620 feet on the Oregon side of the Columbia River Gorge near Troutdale.

RIGHT: Wind and water have sculpted sand and stone at Shore Acres State Park near Coos Bay.

BELOW: The sun sets over Yaquina Harbor at Yaquina Bay in Newport.

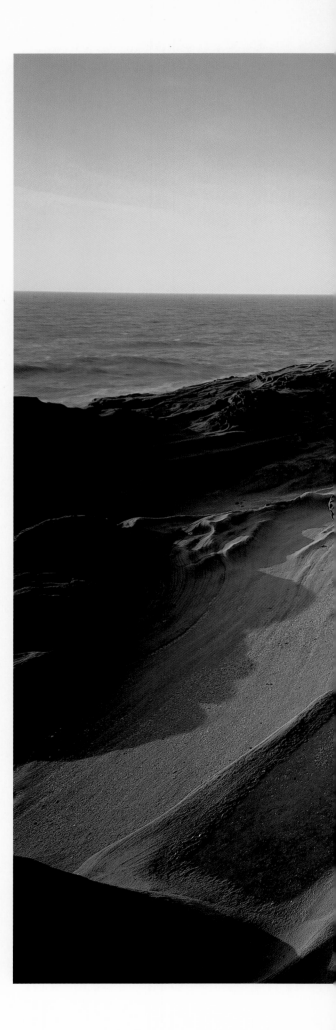

ABOVE: Clematis is reflected through beads of water on the twisting tendrils of a passion flower.

FACING PAGE: A fiery sunrise heralds a new day along the Brownlee Reservoir on the Snake River near Richland.

ABOVE: A snowy road invites winter recreationists to Deschutes National Forest.

RIGHT: South Sister Mountain and Sparks Lake greet a calm winter morning.

ABOVE: Below the Wallowa Mountains near Baker City, fields of wheat and mustard ripple in the breeze.

FACING PAGE: A family fishes Quartzville Creek just off the Quartzville Back Country Byway.

RIGHT: From her high nest perch, a bald eagle carefully watches her young. PHOTO BY TOM AND PAT LEESON

BELOW: Near Astoria stands a reconstruction of Fort Clatsop, where the Lewis and Clark Expedition spent the winter of 1805–1806.

FACING PAGE: Trees and grasses flame with fall color along the North Umpqua River.

Winter snow covers Three-Fingered Jack Mountain, which juts skyward between Mt. Washington and Mt. Jefferson east of Salem.

A tangle of cattails grows along a pond on the Summer Lake State Wildlife Refuge.

ABOVE: Sea lions live all along the Oregon coast. PHOTO BY TOM AND PAT LEESON

LEFT: Cape Perpetua hikers are rewarded with this long-distance view of the Pacific coast.

RIGHT: Remote Wildhorse Lake shimmers below Steens Mountain in the southeastern corner of the state.

BELOW: Reenactors portray life on the Oregon Trail at the National Historic Oregon Trail Interpretive Center in Baker City.

Ice still clings to these rocks in royal-blue Waldo Lake in the Waldo Lake Wilderness.

Hot air balloons ascend into the sky at the Art and Air Festival in Albany.

ABOVE: A pronghorn doe and fawn rest momentarily in a grassy meadow.

LEFT: Storm clouds gather over a field of sunflowers at Hells Canyon National Recreation Area.

LEFT: Late-spring snow chills yellow crocus near Corvallis.

BELOW: A gazebo overlooks the Willamette River in Harrisburg.

FACING PAGE: The Columbia River Hotel is nestled among the trees in the shadow of Oregon's tallest and most famous peak, Mt. Hood.

ABOVE: Fluffy clouds form a picture-perfect backdrop for Cape Blanco Lighthouse, Oregon's oldest and highest lighthouse.

FACING PAGE: Wahkeena Falls splashes over moss-covered rocks in the Columbia River Gorge.

ABOVE: Wild rose vines embrace an old fence near Alpine.

RIGHT: Tokatee Falls cascades over a cliff in Umpqua National Forest.

FACING PAGE: An access road winds through the foothills of Hells Canyon National Recreation Area.

Trees along North Santiam River droop under the weight of heavy snow.

It's Christmastime at this shopping mall in Joseph.

ABOVE: Low tide exposes starfish and a colorful seabed.

LEFT: A red morning means storms may soon come to Bandon Beach.

A thunderstorm rages at the end of this solitary road near Hart Mountain.

The dock at Summer Lake Inn, a full-service lodging and recreation
destination in southeastern Oregon, provides a perfect fly fishing spot.

RIGHT: A fence extends toward the ocean at Cape Kiwanda.

BELOW: Small but proud, the Coquille River Lighthouse was decommissioned in 1963 but is still open for tours.

RIGHT: Common teasel, with its distinctive spiny head, grows in a field of purple grass on the banks of the North Powder River.

BELOW: A jet sledder braves the waves at Cape Kiwanda.

FACING PAGE: It's a calm day at one of America's national treasures, Crater Lake.

ABOVE: A colorful array of gourds and flowers flourish in this Springfield garden.

LEFT: The shore of this dried-up lake below Steens Mountain serves as fertile ground for yellow tansy-leaved evening primrose.

RIGHT: Tiger lily blooms in a garden near Alpine.

BELOW: Sunset light colors storm clouds and pond grasses at Summer Lake.

FACING PAGE: Morning light illuminates the Powder River.

ABOVE: A float plane docks on the Columbia River in the town of Hood River.

FACING PAGE: Whale-watching boats await the migratory animals off the coast near Whale Cove.

LEFT: A salmon heads upstream during the annual migration. PHOTO BY TOM AND PAT LEESON

BELOW: Lupine lines a primitive road near Lakeview.

FACING PAGE: A small stream meets the Pacific Ocean near Cape Blanco.

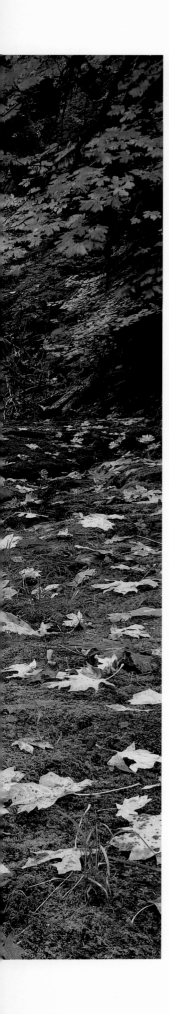

ABOVE: Cattle graze in a green pasture near Alpine.

LEFT: The wind scatters colorful maple leaves around the North Fork of Silver Creek in Silver Falls State Park.

ABOVE: Belly-deep in alfalfa, a buck surveys his surroundings.

RIGHT: Todd Lake shimmers below 9,065-foot Mt. Bachelor in the Three Sisters Wilderness.

ABOVE: A school of rainbow trout glides through the waters of the fish hatchery at Cascade Locks.

FACING PAGE: Below Broken Top Mountain is one of the few remaining glaciers in the continental United States.

ABOVE: The grapes are ripe at Alpine Vineyards.

FACING PAGE: A lone hiker enjoys a view of Drift Creek Falls in the Coast Range.

ABOVE: A bull elk comes out to feed in the evening light. PHOTO BY TOM AND PAT LEESON

RIGHT: Sunset paints a golden scene in the Tom McCall Preserve section of the Columbia River Gorge National Scenic Area.

Forested hills, a sandy beach, and a magnificent ocean view welcome visitors to Humbug Mountain State Park.

This pioneer cabin near Burns recalls the homestead movement
that brought thousands of emigrants to Oregon Territory.

LEFT: The vista from Dee Wright Observatory on McKenzie Pass encompasses lava fields, mountain ridges, and trees crooked with age.

BELOW: A mountain lion looks around as it crosses a small stream. PHOTO BY TOM AND PAT LEESON

ABOVE: Spring flora frames Punch Bowl Falls on Eagle Creek.

FACING PAGE: Indian paintbrush blooms in the shade of Three-Fingered Jack Mountain.

ABOVE: These multihued big-leaf maple leaves all fell from the same tree.

LEFT: Smith Rock State Park, shown here at sunrise, is popular with hikers and rock climbers.

ABOVE: Car tracks cross the cracked surface of Alvord Desert, part of the high desert terrain of southeastern Oregon.

FACING PAGE: Balsamroot and lupine decorate a meadow in the Columbia River National Scenic Area.

LEFT: A young couple delights in a special moment on a park bench as the sun sets over Seaside Beach.

BELOW: Old-growth Ponderosa pines stand tall on the shore of Delintment Lake.

ABOVE: Dahlias bloom in a variety of shades at Shore Acres Botanical Garden.

FACING PAGE: A hang glider comes in for a landing on a sandy hill at Cape Kiwanda.

A rustic chimney is all that remains of this former stagecoach stop near Summer Lake.

ABOVE: A big-leaf maple displays flaming fall color near Monroe.

LEFT: Aptly named Haystack Rock is silhouetted by the sunset at Cape Kiwanda.

ABOVE: This year's alfalfa crop grows among bales from last year's harvest in Malhuer County near Jordan Valley.

FACING PAGE: Flowering gorse blooms bright yellow on a cliff above Bandon Beach.

ABOVE: A California bighorn sheep ram shows off his characteristic spiral horns.

LEFT: Sheep Rock, with its black basalt cap, is a prominent landmark in the John Day Fossil Beds National Monument.

RIGHT: A male elephant seal barks to warn adversaries to stay out of his territory. PHOTO BY GENE AND JASON STONE

BELOW: The whaling vessel *Mary D. Hune*, now moored at Gold Beach, once carried to San Francisco the most valuable shipment of whale oil ever.

Roaring River roars through autumn color along the Aufderheide National Scenic Byway.

ABOVE: Blooming lupine and bear grass mean spring has finally arrived at 4,817-foot Santiam Pass.

FACING PAGE: Strawberry Mountain is reflected in a lake in the rugged Strawberry Mountain Wilderness.

PRECEDING PAGES: The Pacific Coast Highway snakes along the coast south of Cape Sebastian.

LEFT: A recent snow has turned the South Falls area of Silver Falls State Park into a winter wonderland.

BELOW: Spring snowfall still blankets the Wallowa Mountains of northeastern Oregon.

Vine maple is able to survive among these lava blocks from long-ago volcanic explosions.

A young black bear watches from the safety of a tree limb.

PHOTO BY TOM AND PAT LEESON

The High Desert Museum in Bend features exhibits and information about the region's history, culture, and wildlife.

ABOVE: Ocean waves crash and swirl in this hollow rock formation called Devil's Punch Bowl.

FACING PAGE: Quartzville Creek, designated as a National Wild and Scenic River, is protected by the Bureau of Land Management but open to fishing and recreational mining.

ABOVE: Large and natural Klamath Marsh serves as habitat for waterfowl.

FACING PAGE: The timber-lined Moiser Twin Tunnels were recently restored and reopened for use by pedestrians and bicyclists.

Fall color is in full splendor along the banks of the Metolius River.

LEFT: Oregon white oak leaves and acorns float on the surface of a pond near Alpine.

BELOW: An abandoned homestead remembers days past at the base of the Wallowa Mountains near Halfway.

Big Lake reflects the snowy peak of Mt. Washington.

RIGHT: Historic metal signs decorate the side of this barn near Monroe.

BELOW: A decorative porch welcomes visitors to this home in Astoria.

FACING PAGE: This Leslie Gulch road leads intrepid drivers through a maze of colorful rock formations.

ABOVE: Heceta Head, a working lighthouse since 1894, is one of the most-photographed lighthouses in the world.

FACING PAGE: Fog obscures the banks of Lake Billy Chinook, a manmade body of water at the confluence of the Metolius, Deschutes, and Crooked Rivers.

A seagull gets splashed by high waves during a storm at Cape Perpetua.

Sea anemones congregate on the rocky shoreline of Cape Perpetua.

LEFT: A mid-November snow freezes these yellow apples at Summer Lake Inn.

BELOW: Christmas decorations garnish an old truck near Troy.

The Siskiyou National Forest in the Klamath Mountains is covered with snow for much of the year.

Storm clouds roll in over Leslie Gulch, a dry and craggy area in the southeastern part of the state.

LEFT: The sun begins to set over the Crooked River near Prineville.

BELOW: A beaver carries a willow limb into a pond for later feasting. PHOTO BY TOM AND PAT LEESON

ABOVE: Dee Wright Observatory, made of lava rock, offers splendid views of South Sister Mountain at McKenzie Pass.

FACING PAGE: Near Monroe, a lone horse grazes under a cloudy sky.

ABOVE: Azalea petals appear in soft shades of pink and orange.

RIGHT: Malheur National Wildlife Refuge, near Princeton, is a popular birdwatching location.

A Ponderosa pine leans toward the North Fork of the John Day River.

ABOVE: Tufts of azaleas line the walkway at the Japanese Gardens in Portland.

FOLLOWING PAGE: The beautiful coastline of Oregon beckons visitors from all over the world.